★ *A Daily Journal of Gratitude & Love* ★

NICK KEOMAHAVONG

DEDICATION

This journal is dedicated to the best friends who have selflessly provided support, inspiration, and unconditional love.

★ *PERSONAL MESSAGE* ★

TO:
FROM:

Date:_________________   Day #___________

I LOVE YOU BECAUSE...

Date:_______________________   Day #_______________

I LOVE YOU BECAUSE...

Date:_________________   Day #_________

I LOVE YOU BECAUSE...

Date:_________________   Day #_________________

I LOVE YOU BECAUSE...

____

____

____

____

____

____

____

____

____

____

____

____

Date:_______________   Day #_______________

I LOVE YOU BECAUSE...

Date:_______________   Day #_______________

I LOVE YOU BECAUSE...

Date:_______________   Day #_________

I LOVE YOU BECAUSE...

Date:_________________________   Day #__________________

I LOVE YOU BECAUSE...

Date:________________   Day #_____________

I LOVE YOU BECAUSE...

Date:____________________   Day #__________

I LOVE YOU BECAUSE...

Date:_______________   Day #_____________

I LOVE YOU BECAUSE...

Date:________________ Day #__________

I LOVE YOU BECAUSE...

Date:____________________   Day #____________

I LOVE YOU BECAUSE...

Date:_________________   Day #_____________

I LOVE YOU BECAUSE...

Date:_______________   Day #__________

I LOVE YOU BECAUSE...

Date:________________   Day #__________

I LOVE YOU BECAUSE...

Draw the feeling...

Date:__________________   Day #__________

I LOVE YOU BECAUSE...

Date:___________________   Day #___________________

I LOVE YOU BECAUSE...

Date:_________________   Day #_____________

I LOVE YOU BECAUSE...

Date:__________________   Day #__________________

I LOVE YOU BECAUSE...

Date:_________________   Day #_________

I LOVE YOU BECAUSE...

Date:_______________   Day #_______________

I LOVE YOU BECAUSE...

Date:_______________   Day #__________

I LOVE YOU BECAUSE...

Date:_______________   Day #_____________

I LOVE YOU BECAUSE...

Date:_______________________   Day #__________

I LOVE YOU BECAUSE...

Date:_______________   Day #__________

I LOVE YOU BECAUSE...

Date:_________________   Day #_________________

I LOVE YOU BECAUSE...

Date:_________________   Day #___________

I LOVE YOU BECAUSE...

Date:_________________   Day #___________

I LOVE YOU BECAUSE...

Date:_______________   Day #__________

I LOVE YOU BECAUSE...

Date:_________________   Day #_____________

I LOVE YOU BECAUSE...

Date:________________   Day #__________

I LOVE YOU BECAUSE...

Date:_______________________   Day #___________

I LOVE YOU BECAUSE...

Date:_________________ Day #_________

I LOVE YOU BECAUSE...

Date:_________________   Day #_____________

I LOVE YOU BECAUSE...

Date:________________   Day #____________

I LOVE YOU BECAUSE...

Date:________________   Day #__________

I LOVE YOU BECAUSE...

Draw the feeling...

Date:___________________   Day #___________

I LOVE YOU BECAUSE...

____

____

____

____

____

____

____

____

____

____

____

____

____

____

Date:_________________   Day #_____________

I LOVE YOU BECAUSE...

Date:____________________ Day #____________

I LOVE YOU BECAUSE...

Date:_________________   Day #_________________

I LOVE YOU BECAUSE...

Date:_______________________   Day #__________

I LOVE YOU BECAUSE...

Date:____________________   Day #__________

I LOVE YOU BECAUSE...

Date:_____________________ Day #_____________________

I LOVE YOU BECAUSE...

Date:_________________   Day #_____________

I LOVE YOU BECAUSE...

____

____

____

____

____

____

____

____

____

____

____

____

Date:_______________   Day #_______________

I LOVE YOU BECAUSE...

Date:_______________   Day #_______________

I LOVE YOU BECAUSE...

Date:

Day #

I LOVE YOU BECAUSE...

Draw the feeling...

Date:_________________   Day #_____________

I LOVE YOU BECAUSE...

Date:_______________   Day #_______________

I LOVE YOU BECAUSE...

I LOVE YOU BECAUSE...

Date:_________________   Day #________

I LOVE YOU BECAUSE...

Date:_______________   Day #_______________

I LOVE YOU BECAUSE...

Date:_______________________   Day #_______________________

I LOVE YOU BECAUSE...

Date:_______________   Day #_________

I LOVE YOU BECAUSE...

Date:________________   Day #___________

I LOVE YOU BECAUSE...

Date:________________________   Day #________________

I LOVE YOU BECAUSE...

Date:_______________________   Day #_______________________

I LOVE YOU BECAUSE...

Date:_________________   Day #_____________

I LOVE YOU BECAUSE...

____

____

____

____

____

____

____

____

____

____

____

____

Date:________________   Day #__________

I LOVE YOU BECAUSE...

Date:_______________   Day #_______________

I LOVE YOU BECAUSE...

Date:_________________ Day #____________

I LOVE YOU BECAUSE...

Date:_______________   Day #_______________

I LOVE YOU BECAUSE...

Date:_________________   Day #_____________

I LOVE YOU BECAUSE...

Date:_________________   Day #_________________

I LOVE YOU BECAUSE...

Date:_________________   Day #_____________

I LOVE YOU BECAUSE...

____

____

____

____

____

____

____

____

____

____

____

____

____

Date:_________________   Day #___________

I LOVE YOU BECAUSE...

Date:_______________   Day #_____________

I LOVE YOU BECAUSE...

Date:_________________   Day #_________________

I LOVE YOU BECAUSE...

____

____

____

____

____

____

____

____

____

____

____

Date:_______________   Day #___________

I LOVE YOU BECAUSE...

Date:______________________   Day #______________

I LOVE YOU BECAUSE...

Date:_______________   Day #_______________

I LOVE YOU BECAUSE...

Date:_________________   Day #_____________

I LOVE YOU BECAUSE...

Date:_______________   Day #_____________

I LOVE YOU BECAUSE...

Date:_______________   Day #___________

I LOVE YOU BECAUSE...

Date:_________________   Day #__________

I LOVE YOU BECAUSE...

I LOVE YOU BECAUSE...

Date:_______________ Day #_______________

I LOVE YOU BECAUSE...

Date:_________________ Day #__________

I LOVE YOU BECAUSE...

Date:_________________   Day #_________________

I LOVE YOU BECAUSE...

Date:_______________   Day #__________

I LOVE YOU BECAUSE...

Date:_______________   Day #_______________

I LOVE YOU BECAUSE...

Date:

Day #

I LOVE YOU BECAUSE...

Draw the feeling...

Date:_______________   Day #_______________

I LOVE YOU BECAUSE...

Date:_________________   Day #_________________

I LOVE YOU BECAUSE...

Date:_______________   Day #_______________

I LOVE YOU BECAUSE...

Date:_________________________   Day #_____________

I LOVE YOU BECAUSE...

____

____

____

____

____

____

____

____

____

____

____

____

____

Date:________________   Day #_____________

I LOVE YOU BECAUSE...

Date:________________________   Day #____________

I LOVE YOU BECAUSE...

Date:_________________   Day #_______________

I LOVE YOU BECAUSE...

Date:_______________   Day #_____________

I LOVE YOU BECAUSE...

Date:_______________   Day #_______________

I LOVE YOU BECAUSE...

Date:_________________ Day #_________________

I LOVE YOU BECAUSE...

Date:_________________________   Day #_____________________

I LOVE YOU BECAUSE...

Date:_______________ Day #_______________

I LOVE YOU BECAUSE...

Date:_________________   Day #__________

I LOVE YOU BECAUSE...